Ernest Lawrence Thayer

CASEY AT THE BAT

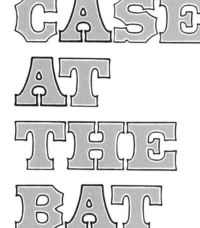

Illustrated by
Jim Hull

With an introduction by
Martin Gardner

Dover Publications, Inc., New York

To Susie
My Beautiful Wife

J. H.

Published in Canada by General Publishing Company, Ltd.,
30 Lesmill Road, Don Mills, Toronto, Ontario.
Published in the United Kingdom by Constable and
Company, Ltd.

This Dover edition, first published in 1977, is a new edition of the poem by Ernest Lawrence Thayer. The illustrations were drawn especially for the Dover edition by Jim
Hull. The Introduction by Martin Gardner originally appeared
in *The Annotated Casey at the Bat*, published in 1967 by
Bramhall House, New York.

International Standard Book Number: 0-486-23461-4
Library of Congress Catalog Card Number: 76-48575

Manufactured in the United States of America
Dover Publications, Inc.
180 Varick Street
New York, N.Y. 10014

Introduction

One of the most humiliating defeats in the history of the New York Yankees took place on Sunday, October 6, 1963. Because a well-thrown ball bounced off the wrist of first baseman Joe Pepitone, the Yanks lost the fourth straight game and the World Series to their old enemies, the former Brooklyn (but by then the Los Angeles) Dodgers. Across the top of next morning's *New York Herald Tribune* ran the headline: "The Mighty Yankees Have Struck Out." Lower on the same page another headline read: "But There's Still Joy in Mudville." (The New York Stock Exchange was holding up well under the grim news.)

Every reader of those headlines knew that they came straight out of that immortal baseball ballad, that masterpiece of humorous verse, *Casey at the Bat*. Not one in ten thousand could have named the man who wrote that poem.

His name was Ernest Lawrence Thayer. The story of how young Thayer, at the age of twenty-five and fresh out of Harvard, wrote *Casey*, and how the ballad became famous, has been told before. But it has seldom been told accurately or in much detail and, in any case, it is worth telling again.

Thayer was born in Lawrence, Massachusetts, on August 14, 1863, exactly one hundred years before the mighty Yankees made their celebrated strike out. By the time he entered Harvard, the family had moved to Worcester where Edward Davis Thayer, Ernest's well-to-do father, ran one of his several woolen mills. At Harvard, young Thayer made a brilliant record as a major in philosophy. William James was both his teacher and friend. Thayer wrote the annual Hasty Pudding play. He was a member of the Delta Kappa Epsilon fraternity and the highly exclusive Fly Club. He edited the Harvard *Lampoon*, the college's humor magazine. Samuel E. Winslow, captain of the senior baseball team (later he became a congressman from Massachusetts), was young Thayer's best friend. During his last year at Harvard, Thayer never missed a ball game.

Another friend of Thayer's college years was the *Lampoon's* business manager, William Randolph Hearst. In 1885, when Thayer was graduated *magna cum laude*—he was Phi Beta Kappa and the Ivy orator of his class—Hearst was unceremoniously booted off the Harvard Yard. (He had a habit of playing practical jokes that no one on the faculty thought funny, such as sending chamber pots to professors, their names inscribed thereon.) Hearst's father had recently bought the ailing *San Francisco Examiner* to promote his candidacy as United States senator from California. Now that young Will was in want of something to occupy his time, the elder Hearst turned the paper over to him.

Thayer, in the meantime, after wandering around Europe with no particular goal, settled in Paris to brush up on his French. Would he consider, Hearst cabled him, returning to the United States to write a humor column for the *Examiner's* Sunday supplement? To the great annoyance of his father, who expected him to take over the American Woolen Mills someday, Thayer accepted Hearst's offer.

Thayer's contributions to the paper began in 1886. Most were unsigned, but starting in October, 1887 and continuing into December he wrote a series of ballads that ran in the Sunday editions, about every other week, under the by-line of "Phin." (At Harvard his friends had called him Phinny.) Then ill health forced him to return to Worcester. He continued for a while to send material to the *Examiner,* including one final ballad, *Casey.* It appeared on Sunday, June 3, 1888, page 4, column 4, sandwiched inconspicuously between editorials on the left and a weekly column by Ambrose Bierce on the right.

No one paid much attention to *Casey.* Baseball fans in San Francisco chuckled over it and a few eastern papers reprinted it, but it could have been quickly forgotten had it not been for a sequence of improbable events. In New York City a rising young comedian and bass singer, William De Wolf Hopper, was appearing in *Prince Methusalem,* a comic opera at Wallack's Theatre, at Broadway and 30th Street. One evening (the exact date is unknown; it was probably late in 1888 or early in 1889) James Mutrie's New York Giants and Pop Anson's Chicago White Stockings were invited to the show as guests of the management. What could he do on stage, Hopper asked himself, for the special benefit of these men? I have just the thing, said Archibald Clavering Gunter, a novelist and friend. He took from his pocket a ragged newspaper clipping that he had cut from the *Examiner* on a recent trip to San Francisco. It was *Casey.*

This, insisted Gunter, is great. Why not memorize it and deliver it on stage? Hopper did exactly that, in the middle of the second act, with the Giants in boxes on one side of the theatre, the White Stockings in boxes on the other. This is how Hopper recalled the scene in his memoirs, *Once a Clown Always a Clown:*

When I dropped my voice to B flat, below low C, at "the multitude was awed," I remember seeing Buck Ewing's gallant mustachios give a single nervous twitch. And as the house, after a moment of startled silence, grasped the anticlimactic dénouement, it shouted its glee.

They had expected, as any one does on hearing Casey for the first time, that the mighty batsman would slam the ball out of the lot, and a lesser bard would have had him do so, and thereby written merely a good sporting-page filler. The crowds do not flock into the American League parks around the circuit when the Yankees play, solely in anticipation of seeing Babe Ruth whale the ball over the centerfield fence. That is a spectacle to be enjoyed even at the expense of the home team, but there always is a chance that the Babe will strike out, a sight even more healing to sore eyes, for the Sultan of Swat can miss the third strike just as furiously as he can meet it, and the contrast between the terrible threat of his swing and the futility of the result is a banquet for the malicious, which includes

us all. There is no more completely satisfactory drama in literature than the fall of Humpty Dumpty.

Astonished and delighted with the way his audience responded to *Casey,* Hopper made the recitation a permanent part of his repertoire. It became his most famous bit. Wherever he went, whatever the show in which he was appearing, there were always curtain shouts for "Casey!" By his own count he recited it more than 10,000 times, experimenting with hundreds of slight variations in emphasis and gesture to keep his mind from wandering. It took him exactly five minutes and forty seconds to deliver the poem.

"When my name is called upon the resurrection morning," he wrote in his memoirs, "I shall, very probably, unless some friend is there to pull the sleeve of my ascension robes, arise, clear my throat and begin: 'The outlook wasn't brilliant for the Mudville nine that day.'" The poem, declared Hopper, is the only truly great comic poem written by an American.

It is as perfect an epitome of our national game today as it was when every player drank his coffee from a mustache cup. There are one or more Caseys in every league, bush or big, and there is no day in the playing season that this same supreme tragedy, as stark as Aristophanes for the moment, does not befall on some field. It is unique in all verse in that it is not only funny and ironic, but excitingly dramatic, with the suspense built up to a perfect climax. There is no lame line among the fifty-two.

Let us pause for some moments of irony. Although Hopper was famous in his day as a comic-opera star, today he is remembered for three things: 1) Hedda Hopper was the fifth of his six wives; 2) William Hopper, his only child by Hedda, played Paul Drake in the Perry Mason TV show; and 3) He was the man who recited *Casey.*

More ironic still, Gunter—who wrote thirty-nine novels including a best seller called *Mr. Barnes of New York*—has found his way into terrestrial immortality only because he happened to take *Casey* out of a newspaper and pass it on to Hopper. We must not belittle this achievement. "It is easy enough to recognize a masterpiece after it has been carefully cleaned and beautifully framed and hung in a conspicuous place and certified by experts," wrote Burton Stevenson, a critic and poetry anthologist, with specific reference to Gunter and *Casey.* "But to stumble over it in a musty garret, covered with dust, to dig it out of a pile of junk and know it for a thing of beauty—only the connoisseur can do that."

Gunter was the connoisseur, but Hopper made the poem famous. All over the United States, newspapers and magazines began to reprint it. No one knew who "Phin" was. Editors either dropped the name altogether, or substituted their own or a fictitious one. Stanzas were lost. Lines got botched by printers or rewritten by editors who fancied themselves able to improve the original. Scarcely two printings of the poem were the same. In one early reprinting, by the *New York Sporting Times,* July 29, 1888, Mudville was changed to Boston and Casey's name to Kelly, in honor of Mike ("King") Kelly, a famous Chicago star who had recently been bought by the Boston team.

After the banquet at a Harvard decennial class reunion in 1895, Thayer recited *Casey* and delivered an eloquent speech, tinged with ironic humor and sadness. (It is printed, along with *Casey,* in *Harvard University, Class of 1885: Secretary's Report No. V,* 1900, pp. 88–96.) The burden of his address was that the world turns out to be not quite the bowl of cherries that a haughty Harvard undergraduate expects it to be. Surely the following passage is but a roundabout way of saying that it is easy to strike out:

We give today a wider and larger application to that happy phrase of the jury box, "extenuating circumstances." We have found that playing the game is very different from watching it played, and that splendid theories, even when accepted by the combatants, are apt to be lost sight of in the confusion of active battle.

We have reached an age, those of us to whom fortune has assigned a post in life's struggle, when, beaten and smashed and biffed by the lashings of the dragon's tail, we begin to appreciate that the old man was not such a damned fool after all. We saw our parents wrestling with that same dragon, and we thought, though we never spoke the thought aloud, "Why don't he hit him on the head?" Alas, comrades, we know now. We have hit the dragon on the head and we have seen the dragon smile.

From time to time various "Caseys" who actually played baseball in the late 1880's claimed to have been the inspiration for the ballad. But Thayer emphatically denied that he had had any ball player in mind for any of the men mentioned in *Casey.* When the *Syracuse Post-Standard* wrote to ask him about this, he replied with a letter that is reprinted in full in Lee Allen's entertaining book on baseball, *The Hot Stove League:*

The verses owe their existence to my enthusiasm for college baseball, not as a player, but as a fan. . . . The poem has no basis in fact. The only Casey actually involved—I am sure about him—was not a ball player. He was a big, dour Irish lad of my high school days. While in high school, I composed and printed myself a very tiny sheet, less than two inches by three. In one issue, I ventured to gag, as we say, this Casey boy. He didn't like it and he told me so, and, as he discoursed, his big, clenched, red hands were white at the knuckles. This Casey's name never again appeared in the *Monohippic Gazette.* But I suspect the incident, many years after, suggested the title for the poem. It was a taunt thrown to the winds. God grant he never catches me.

By 1900 almost everyone in America had heard or read the poem. No one knew who had written it. For years it was attributed to William Valentine, city editor of the *Sioux City Tribune,* Iowa. One George Whitefield D'Vys, of Cambridge, actually went about proudly proclaiming himself the author; he even signed a document to this effect and had it notarized. In 1902 *A Treasury of Humorous Poetry,* edited by Frederic Lawrence Knowles, credited the poem to someone named Joseph Quinlan

Murphy. To this day no one knows who Murphy might have been, if he really existed, or why Knowles supposed he had written *Casey.*

Hopper himself did not find out who wrote the ballad until about five years after he began reciting it. One evening, having delivered the poem in a Worcester theater, he received a note inviting him to a local club to meet *Casey's* author. "Over the details of wassail that followed," Hopper wrote later, "I will draw a veil of charity." He did disclose, however, that the club members had persuaded Thayer himself to stand up and recite *Casey.* It was, Hopper declared, the worst delivery of the poem he had ever heard. "In a sweet, dulcet Harvard whisper he [Thayer] implored Casey to murder the umpire, and gave this cry of mass animal rage all the emphasis of a caterpillar wearing rubbers crawling on a velvet carpet."

Thayer remained in Worcester for many years, doing his best to please his father by managing one of the family mills. He kept quietly to himself, studying philosophy in spare hours and reading classical literature. He was a slightly built, soft-spoken man, inclined to deafness in his middle years (he wore a hearing aid); always gracious, charming and modest. Although he dashed off four or five more comic ballads in 1896, for Hearst's *New York Journal,* he continued to have a low opinion of his verse.

"During my brief connection with the *Examiner,*" Thayer once wrote,

I put out large quantities of nonsense, both prose and verse, sounding the whole newspaper gamut from advertisements to editorials. In general quality *Casey* (at least in my judgment) is neither better nor worse than much of the other stuff. Its persistent vogue is simply unaccountable, and it would be hard to say, all things considered, if it has given me more pleasure than annoyance. The constant wrangling about the authorship, from which I have tried to keep aloof, has certainly filled me with disgust.

Throughout his life Thayer refused to discuss payments for reprintings of *Casey.* "All I ask is never to be reminded of it again," he told one publisher. "Make it anything you wish."

Never happy with the woolly details of the family mills, Thayer finally quit working for them altogether. After a few years of travel abroad, he retired in 1912 to Santa Barbara, California. The following year—he was then fifty—he married Mrs. Rosalind Buel Hammett, a widow from St. Louis. They had no children.

Thayer remained in Santa Barbara until his death in 1940. Friends said that toward the end of his life he softened a bit in his scornful attitude toward *Casey.* By then even English professors, notably William Lyon Phelps of Yale, had hailed the poem as an authentic native masterpiece. "The psychology of the hero and the psychology of the crowd leave nothing to be desired," wrote Phelps, in *What I Like in Poetry* (Scribner's, 1934).

There is more knowledge of human nature displayed in this poem than in many of the works of the psychiatrist. Furthermore, it is a tragedy of Destiny. There is nothing so stupid as Destiny. It is a centrifugal tragedy, by which our minds are turned from the fate of Casey to the universal. For this is the curse that hangs over humanity—our ability to accomplish any feat is in inverse ratio to the intensity of our desire.

Thayer attended a class reunion at Harvard in 1935. Friends reported that he was visibly touched when he saw a classmate carrying a large banner that read: "An '85 Man Wrote *Casey!*"

Music for Thayer's poem was written by Sidney Homer and published by G. Schirmer, New York City, in 1920. (The sheet music bears the general title: *Six Cheerful Songs to Poems of American Humor.* Casey is No. 3.) Two silent movies were about Casey. The first starred Hopper himself as the mighty batsman. It was produced by Fine Arts-Triangle and released June 22, 1916. (Scenes from this film may be found in *The Triangle,* Vol. 2, June 17, 1916.) A remake, with Wallace Beery in the leading role (supported by Ford Sterling and Zasu Pitts), was released by Paramount on April 17, 1927. I can still recall Beery, bat in one hand and beer mug in the other, whacking the ball so hard that an outfielder had to mount a horse to retrieve it. An animated cartoon of the famous strike out was included in Walt Disney's 1946 release, *Make Mine Music,* with Jerry Colonna providing an off-camera recitation of Thayer's ballad. (Since 1960 this has been available as a reissued short feature from Encyclopaedia Britannica Films.) In 1953 Disney released a cartoon short called *Casey Bats Again.* It tells how Casey organized a girls' baseball team, then, to save the game in a pinch, dressed like a girl and batted in the winning run.

The most important continuation and elaboration of the Casey story is an opera, *The Mighty Casey,* which had its world première in Hartford, Connecticut, on May 4, 1953. William Schuman, who wrote the music, is now the president of New York City's Lincoln Center for the Performing Arts. He has been a baseball buff since his childhood on New York's upper west side. In his teens he seriously considered becoming a professional ball player. "Baseball was my youth," he has written. "Had I been a better catcher, I might never have become a musician." But in his early twenties his love of music won out, and by 1941 (he was then thirty-one) his Third Symphony lifted him into the ranks of major United States composers. From 1935 to 1961 he was president of the Juilliard School of Music, and since 1962 he has been head of Lincoln Center. Jeremy Gury, who wrote *The Mighty Casey's* libretto, was senior vice-president and creative director of Ted Bates & Company, New York City, in 1953. Before he entered advertising he had been managing editor of *Stage Magazine.* He has written a number of children's books (*The Round and Round Horse, The Wonderful World of Aunt Trudy,* and others) and one play (with music by Alex North), *The Hither and Thither of Danny Dither.*

The Mighty Casey obviously is the product of two knowledgeable baseball enthusiasts. They have expanded the Casey myth with such loving insight, such full appreciation of the nuances in Thayer's

ballad, that no Casey fan need hesitate to add the opera to the *Casey* canon. It is sad that Thayer did not live to see it. The details of its plot mesh so smoothly with the poem that one feels at once, "Yes, of course, that *must* have been the way it happened."

The Mighty Casey has yet to have a full-scale production in New York City. (It is not easy to put on a short opera that calls for a forty-piece orchestra and a chorus of fifty voices!) After its one performance in Hartford, there was a CBS television production of *The Mighty Casey* on the Omnibus show, March 6, 1955, and it has been performed by small companies in San Francisco, Annapolis, and elsewhere. There have been several productions in baseball-loving Japan. Harold C. Schonberg, reviewing the Hartford production in *The New York Times* (May 5, 1953, page 34), spoke of the music as "lively, amusing, tongue-in-cheek." He felt that Schuman's "dry, often jerky melodic line with all its major sevenths and ninths, his austere harmonies and his rhythmic intensity," doesn't quite fit Thayer's "pleasant little fable." Can it be that the music critic of *The New York Times* is not a baseball fan? Pleasant little fable, indeed! *Casey* is neither pleasant nor little, it is tragic and titanic. Perhaps Schuman's intense music is not so inappropriate after all.

Several flimsy paperback copies of the poem, with illustrations, were printed around the turn of the century, but it was not until 1964 that *Casey* appeared in handsomely illustrated hardcover editions.

How can one explain *Casey's* undying popularity? It is not great poetry. It was written carelessly. Parts of it are certainly doggerel. Yet it is almost impossible to read it several times without memorizing whole chunks, and there are lines so perfectly expressed, given the poem's intent, that one cannot imagine a word changed for the better. T. S. Eliot admired the ballad and even wrote a parody about a cat, "Growltiger's Last Stand" (a poem in *Old Possum's Book of Practical Cats,* Harcourt, Brace, 1939), in which many of Thayer's lines are echoed.

Introduction

The poem's secret can be found, of all places, in the autobiography of George Santayana, another famous Harvard philosopher. Santayana was one of Thayer's associate editors on the *Lampoon*. "The man who gave the tone to the *Lampoon* at that time," Santayana writes in *Persons and Places* (Scribner's, 1943),

was Ernest Thayer. . . . He seemed a man apart, and his wit was not so much jocular as Mercutio-like, curious and whimsical, as if he saw the broken edges of things that appear whole. There was some obscurity in his play with words, and a feeling (which I shared) that the absurd side of things is pathetic. Probably nothing in his later performance may bear out what I have just said of him, because American life was then becoming unfavorable to idiosyncrasies of any sort, and the current smoothed and rounded out all the odd pebbles.

But Santayana was wrong. One thing *did* bear this out, and that was *Casey*. It is precisely the blend of the absurd and the tragic that lies at the heart of Thayer's remarkable poem. Casey is the giant of baseball who, at his moment of potential triumph, strikes out. A pathetic figure, yet comic because of the supreme arrogance and confidence with which he approached the plate.

There was ease in Casey's manner as he stepped into his place;
There was pride in Casey's bearing and a smile on Casey's face.

And when, responding to the cheers, he lightly doffed his hat,
No stranger in the crowd could doubt 'twas Casey at the bat.

It is the shock of contrast between this beautiful build-up and the final fizzle that produces the poem's explosion point. The story of Casey has become an American myth because Casey is the incomparable, towering symbol of the great and glorious poop-out.

One might argue that Thayer, with his extraordinary beginning at Harvard, his friendship with James and Santayana, his lifelong immersion in philosophy and the great books, was himself something of a Casey. In later years his friends were constantly urging him to write, but he would always shake his head and reply, "I have nothing to say." Not until just before his death, at the age of seventy-seven, did he make an attempt to put some serious thoughts on paper. Then it was too late. "*Now* I have something to say," he said, "and I am too weak to say it.'

But posterity's judgments are hard to anticipate. Thayer's writing career was no strikeout. He swatted one magnificent home run, *Casey at the Bat;* and as long as baseball is played on this old earth, on Mudville, the air will be shattered over and over again by the force of Casey's blow.

Martin Gardner

The outlook wasn't brilliant for the Mudville nine that day;

The score stood four to two with but one inning more to play.

So when Cooney died at second, . . .

. . . and Burrows did the same,

A pallor wreathed the features of the patrons of the game.

A straggling few got up to go in deep despair. The rest

Clung to the hope which springs eternal in the human breast;

They thought, "If only Casey could but get a whack at that——

We'd put up even money now with Casey at the bat."

But Flynn preceded Casey, as did also Jimmy Blake,

And the former was a lulu . . .

. . . and the latter was a fake;

So upon that stricken multitude a deathlike silence sat,

For there seemed but little chance of Casey's getting to the bat.

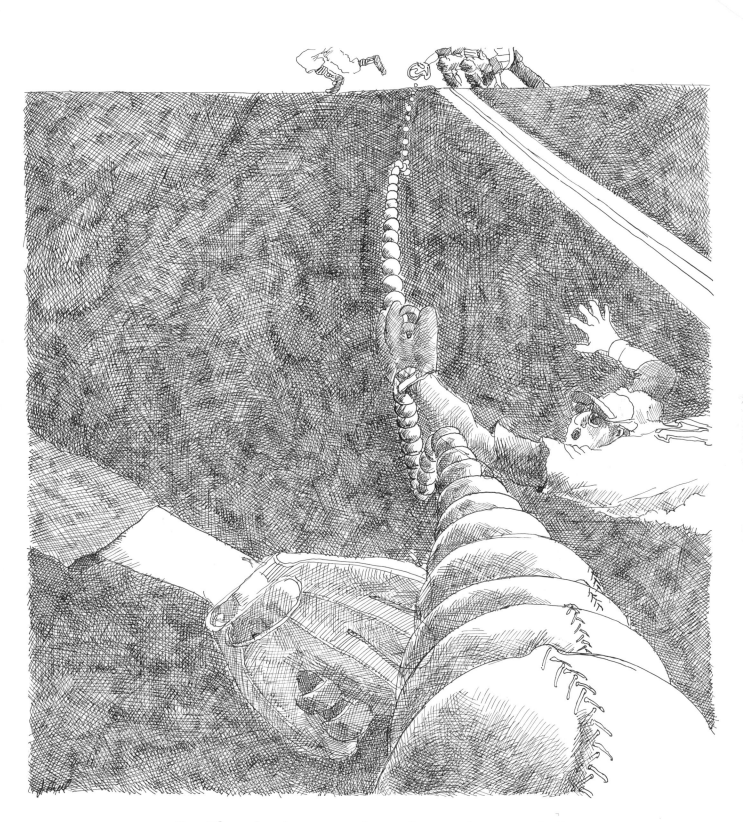

But Flynn let drive a single, to the wonderment of all,

And Blake, the much despis-ed, tore the cover off the ball;

And when the dust had lifted, and the men saw what had occurred,

There was Jimmy safe at second and Flynn a-hugging third.

Then from five thousand throats and more there rose a lusty yell;

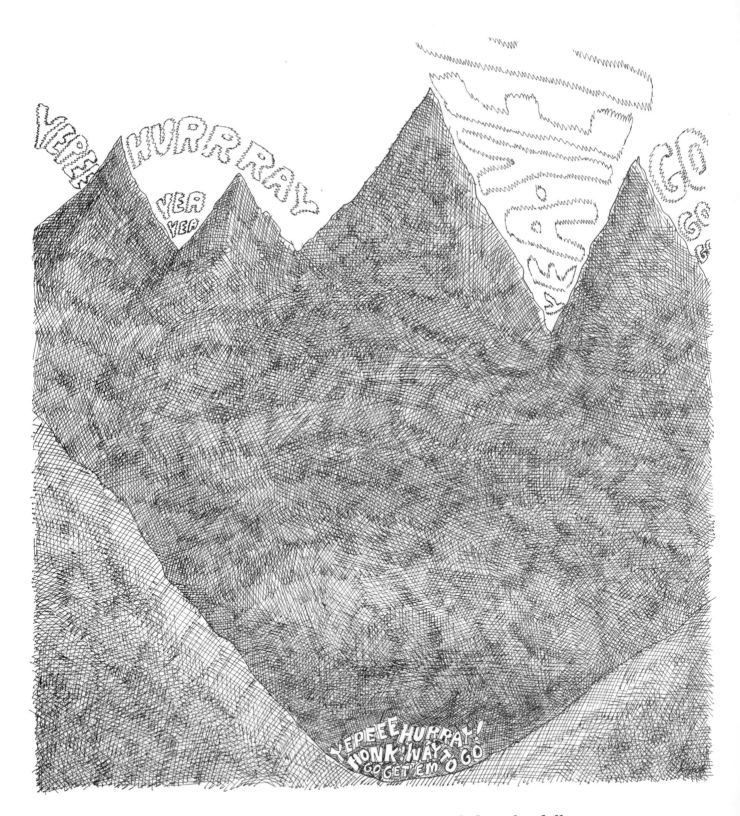

It rumbled in the mountaintops, it rattled in the dell;

It knocked upon the hillside and recoiled upon the flat,

For Casey, mighty Casey, was advancing to the bat.

There was ease in Casey's manner as he stepped into his place;

There was pride in Casey's bearing and a smile on Casey's face.

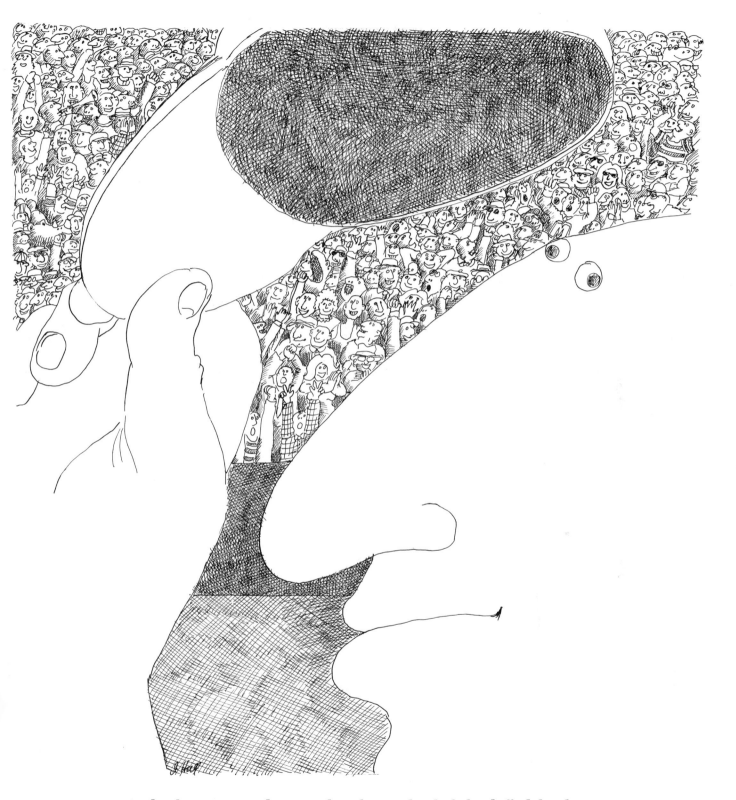

And when, responding to the cheers, he lightly doffed his hat,

No stranger in the crowd could doubt 'twas Casey at the bat.

Ten thousand eyes were on him as he rubbed his hands with dirt;

Five thousand tongues applauded when he wiped them on his shirt.

Then while the writhing pitcher ground the ball into his hip,

Defiance gleamed in Casey's eye, a sneer curled Casey's lip.

And now the leather-covered sphere came hurtling through the air,

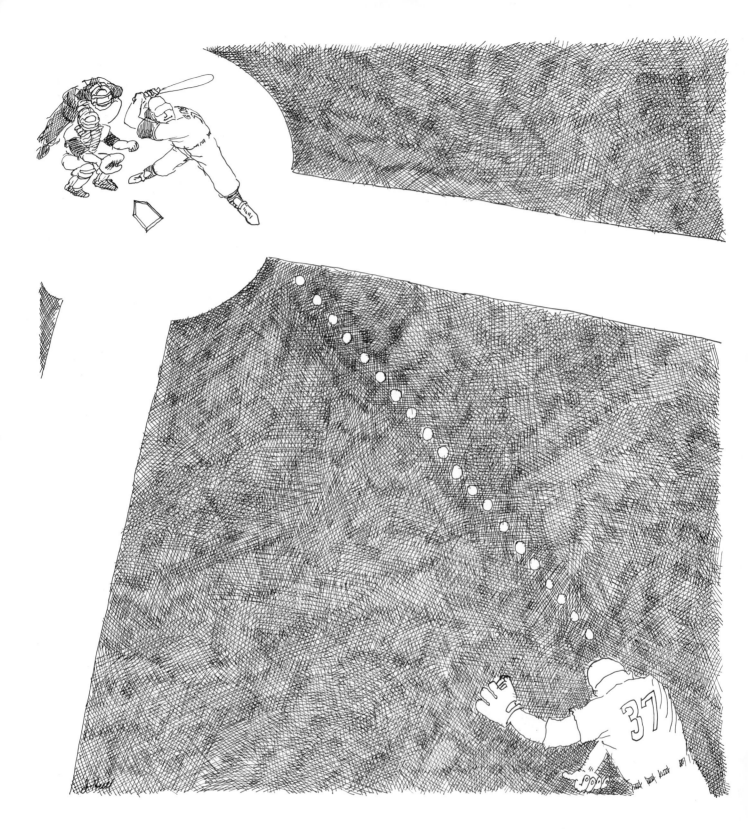

And Casey stood a-watching it in haughty grandeur there.

Close by the sturdy batsman the ball unheeded sped——

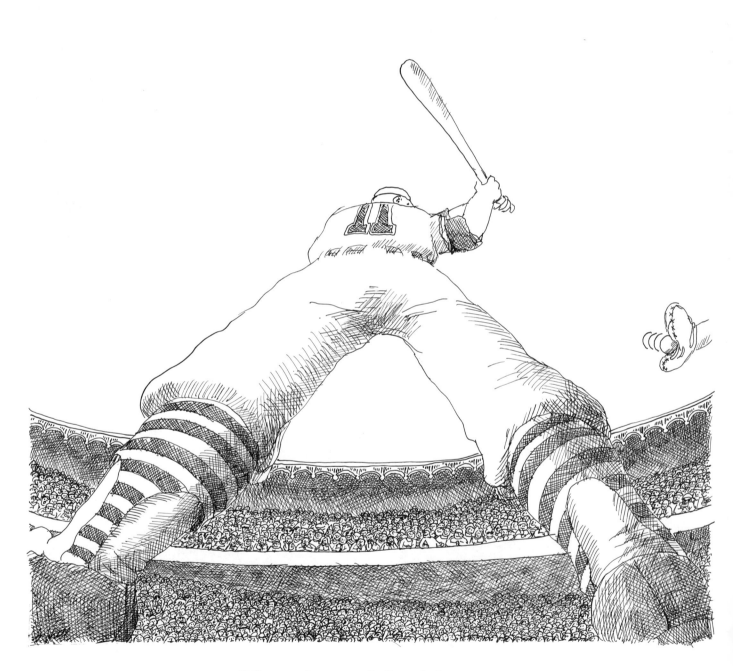

"That ain't my style," said Casey. . . .

. . . "Strike one," the umpire said.

From the benches, black with people, there went up a muffled roar,

Like the beating of the storm-waves on a stern and distant shore.

"Kill him! Kill the umpire!" shouted someone on the stand;

And it's likely they'd have killed him had not Casey raised his hand.

With a smile of Christian charity great Casey's visage shone;

He stilled the rising tumult; he bade the game go on;

He signaled to the pitcher, and once more the spheroid flew;

But Casey still ignored it, and the umpire said, "Strike two."

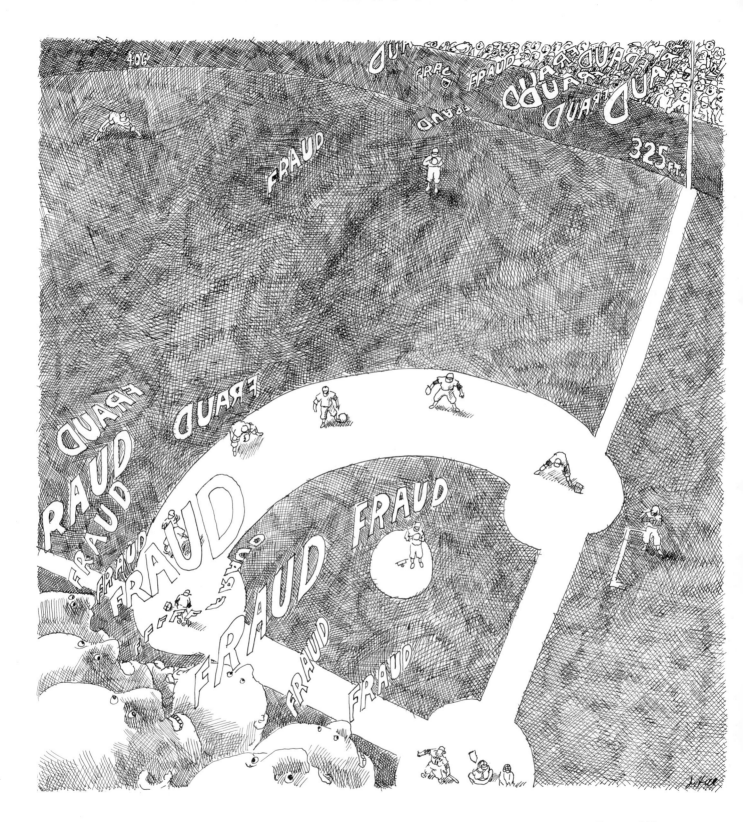

"Fraud!" cried the maddened thousands, and the echo answered, "Fraud!"

But one scornful look from Casey and the multitude was awed.

They saw his face grow stern and cold, they saw his muscles strain,

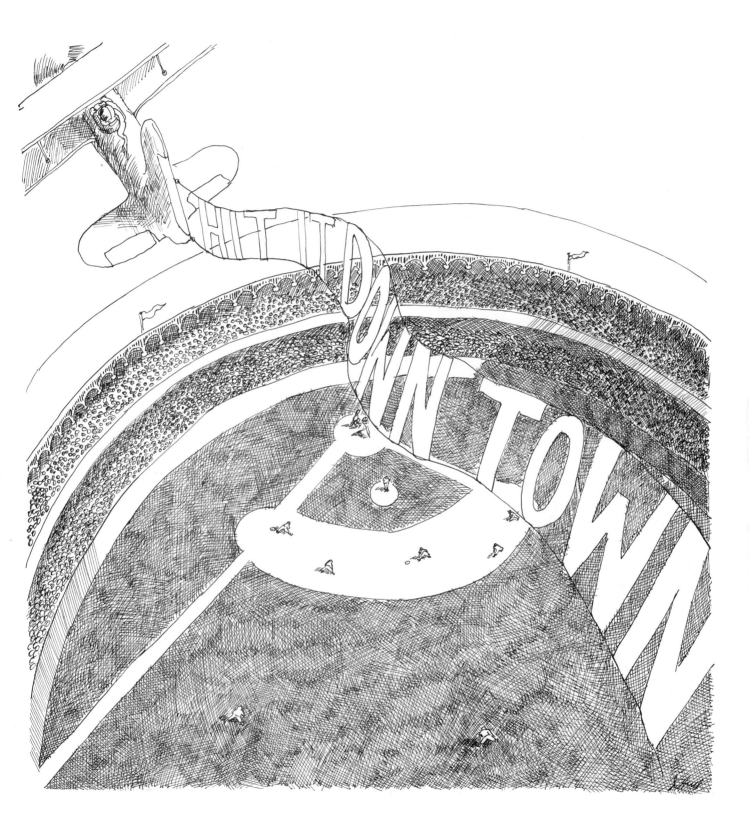

And they knew that Casey wouldn't let that ball go by again.

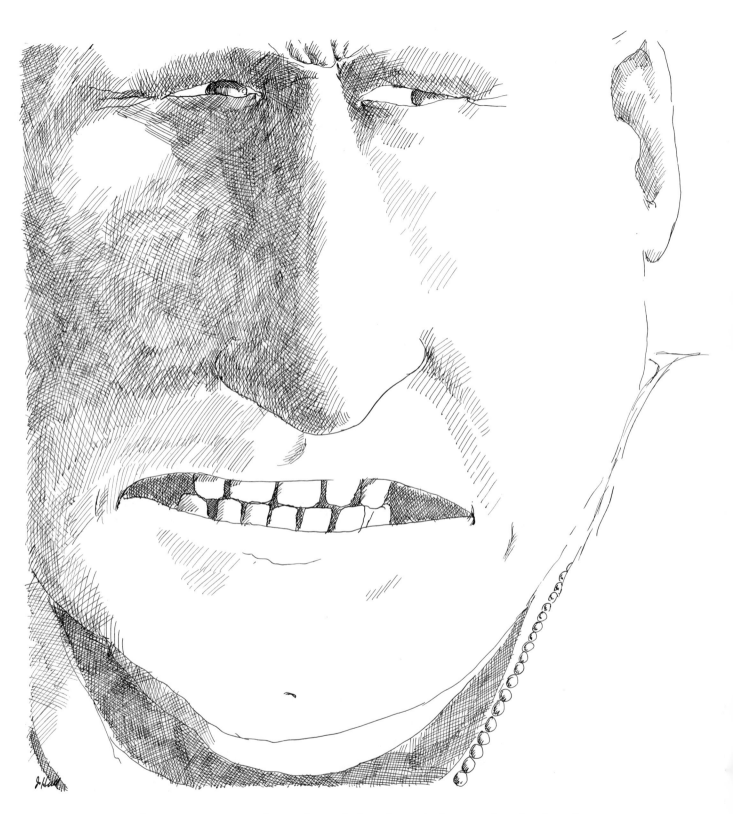

The sneer is gone from Casey's lip, his teeth are clenched in hate;

He pounds with cruel violence his bat upon the plate.

And now the pitcher holds the ball, . . .

. . . and now he lets it go,

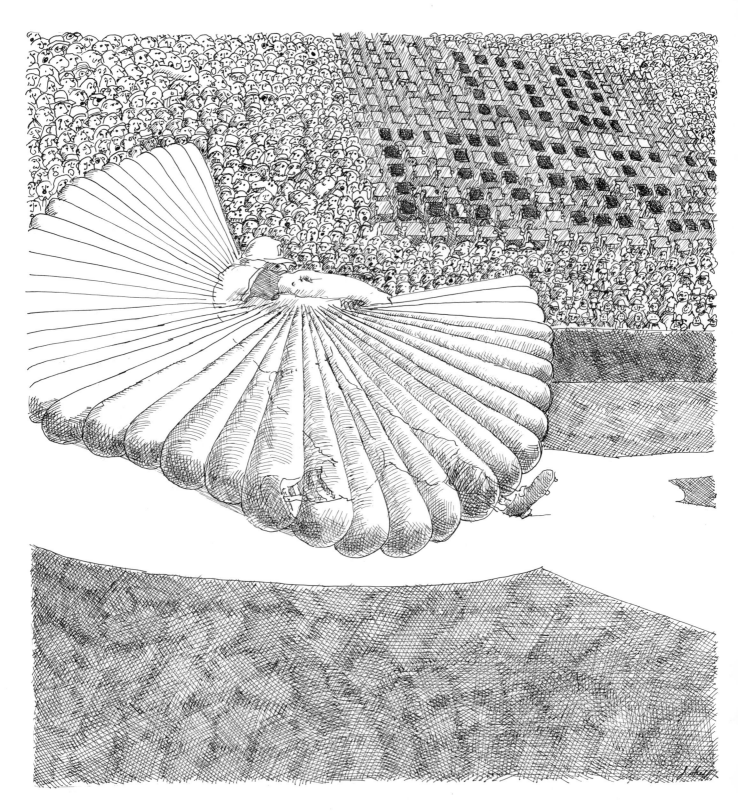

And now the air is shattered by the force of Casey's blow.

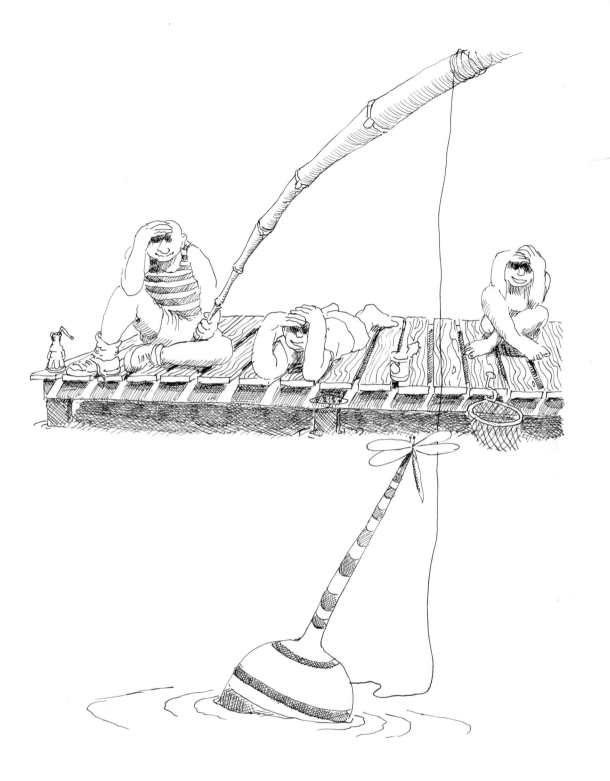

Oh, somewhere in this favored land the sun is shining bright;

The band is playing somewhere, and somewhere hearts are light,

And somewhere men are laughing, and somewhere children shout;

But there is no joy in Mudville—mighty Casey has struck out.